Poetic Stories

ROBERT ROGERS

To order additional copies of this book, contact:
Xlibris
844-714-8691
www.Xlibris.com
Orders@Xlibris.com

ISBN: Softcover   978-1-6641-6016-3
        EBook   978-1-6641-6015-6

Print information available on the last page.

Rev. date: 02/25/2021

Poetic Stories

Her Clothes Came Off

Needed Love

Wild Love

Wanting Love

Robert Rogers

Contents

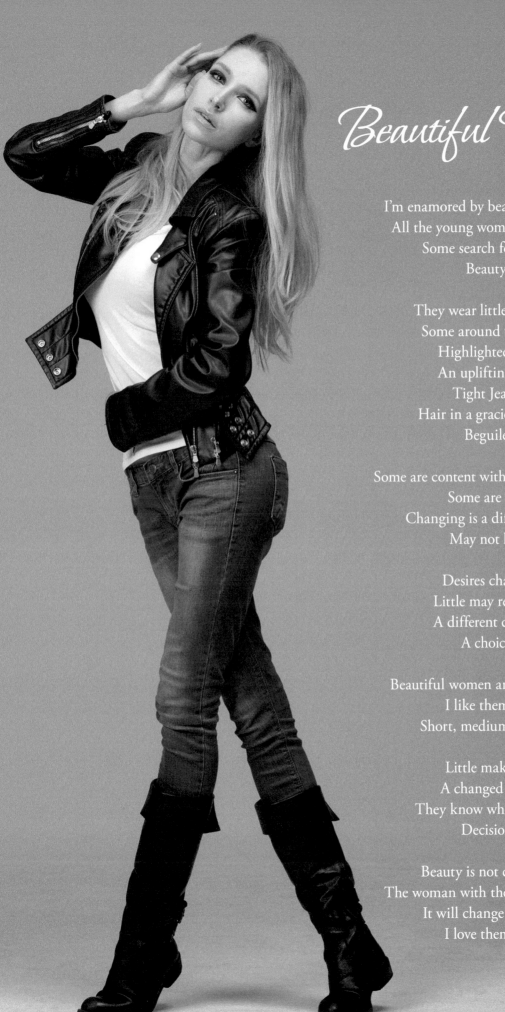

Beautiful Women

I'm enamored by beautiful women
All the young women are pretty
Some search for more
Beauty

They wear little makeup
Some around the eyes
Highlighted lips
An uplifting bra
Tight Jeans
Hair in a gracious style
Beguile

Some are content with what they have
Some are not
Changing is a difficult task
May not last

Desires change
Little may remain
A different course
A choice

Beautiful women are compelling
I like them all
Short, medium, or tall

Little makeup
A changed look
They know what it took
Decision

Beauty is not constant
The woman with the jeans is mine
It will change in time
I love them all

Desperado

Desperado songs
I'm not a cowboy
Just desperate
Want to hear a different song

She drinks
Holds that cigarette to her lips
Wish I had that pleasure
Kiss her

Whisky and smoke are addictive
She relishes the feeling
Brandishes the sight
She can't be right

I have an addiction
It's her

She is a compelling sight
Glows in the night
Seems to know what is right
She can't be right

We all make mistakes
Don't realize what's at stake
I'm the same
It's a dangerous game

I may become a desperado
Endure a desperate life
Listen to a different song
Live without her

Dream World

A woman can be dreamed
Live in the heart of a man
The dream may never come true
Only imagined

We wake to reality
Our dreams are lost
We stumble from the bed
Try to remember what we had

Only brief images remain
I hope she returns
Lives in my dream
Wish she would come true

Can she ever be real?
Know me?

Fulfill my dream
Know how I feel

When I sleep she returns
I want to see her again
Remember her when I wake
Not let that image escape

I've dreamed her a long time
She is only mine
I want to find her
Live the reality
Wish that dream to come true
I live in a dream world

Getting Old

Can't do What I once did
Getting old is a pain
Young I can't remain
It shows in many ways

Struggle out of bed
Fumble with my shoes
Lean against the door
Can't remember what I said

In a naked state
I look down
Hold it
Wish it would rise again

Making love disappeared
What a shame
I remember being young
I feel the same

I stumble down the steps
Hold tight to that coffee cup
It becomes cold
Like my life

I'm not sad
Remember what I had
Want to do what I once did
Tie my shoes

Hold that thing
Feel it rise again
Make love

Her Clothes Came Off

She was singing
Dancing in the kitchen
I just listened
Loved the song

She began taking her clothes off
Kicked the shoes in the living room
Felt better I assume
She watched the pasta steam

What a sight
It seemed alright
We were alone
I just watched

Next came the shirt
The buttons seemed a bit tight
I thought she might be the same
That Margaretta could be to blame

Her hair came down
The skirt followed
I held my breath
Controlled myself

She laid that wood spoon on the floor
Danced around it
Both hands unbuttoned the bra
Enjoyed what I saw

The slip remained tight
That seemed alright
The steam kept her warm
Didn't cause any harm

The rest came off
I smiled and picked up the shoes
What could I choose?
I listened to the song

Waited for the pasta

5

I Am Lost

Light this darkness
Help me see your loving light
Strike a flame
I want to find you

I want to feel your love
Sink deep in my heart
We can love again
Let me love you

I am traveling down an unknown path
Guide me
I want to see the glow in your eyes
See your loving light

Help me
Hold me to your breast
Envelope me
I am lost

You drifted away
I don't know why
I lost you
Show me a new course

Erase my longing
Feel that loving fire
Relish in the warmth
Come Back
Hold my hand

I Need You

I found you
Let me come in
Our love is like this rain
Cold

Let me warm you
I want you
need you
Love me again

I know I've done wrong
I've made mistakes
I want to change
Tell me what it takes

I will sincerely listen
Change
I want to be with you
Be with me

The rain has cleansed the wrong
Know what I can be
A loving man
Please know I can

Help me escape the cold
Live again in your sunshine

I Remember

I remember my wish
I wish I didn't
I remember what you said
It still hurts

I wanted to love you
My wish didn't come true
It simply lingers
Tears at my heart

My life is coming apart
I don't want to remember
You didn't say goodbye
I don't know why

You walked through that door
Stopped
Said I can't love you anymore
You have changed

You wanted to be alone
Forget the past
Your love didn't last
You hurt me

I want to find love
Mend this heart
My wish may come true
I will try not to remember you

Close that remembrance door

I'm Alone

I 'm alone
A stranger

I play the piano
Write songs
Paint pictures
Stay at home
I'm alone

No one shares
I seek a man
Hold his hand
Feel the warmth

I do wish to find him
I want to dream together
Love him
Know I'm not alone

Time will tell
It may fail
Life is strange
May not change
Alone I may remain

I can only hope
Maybe a man will enter my life
Stop this strife
Love me

Alone I remain
May never change
Life is strange
I can only hope

Let Me Love you

I want to love you
You won't let me
You remember the past
That feeling seems to last

I remember the good times
The love we shared
I cared
You have changed

I liked pretty women
I touched
I could see you blush
The cheeks turned red

You turned
Walked away
Nothing to say
You still remember

I was foolish
Thought that blush wouldn't last
Live in the past
I want to love you
You won't let me

You have changed
My care remains
Let us relive that love
I want to

Please let me

Love Is Strange

I do love her
Can't seem to stop
I don't know why
Should I try?

She never listens
My words are dismissed
She gives me a kiss
Smiles and waves

She turns and walks away
I don't know what to say
I Just stand there
Loving her is strange

Will love cease?
Difficult to say
Why?
The kiss lingers

She never listens
My words fade
Never saved
Simply dismissed with that wave

I live with her kiss and wave
My words only I can save
She may remember when she loved me
My words may come together

She will hear them

Loved That Buick

I loved that Buick
It belonged to Dad
The only new one he ever had
Shifting was easy

It was a Sadanett
He let me drive
I took Shelly to the drive-in show
What would follow I didn't know
I just wished

Hung the speaker on the window
Turned the sound up high
Watched John Wayne
I contemplated what to gain

Suggested the back seat
She said no
I thought so
Just wished

I drove to the beach
We sat in the sand
She held my hand
My wish might come true

The engine was still warm
We leaned against the tire
We kissed
Wishes can come true

That back seat played a role
A lasting memory
I loved that car
Shifting was easy

Loving Sex

Met her in the bar
We talked awhile
She was a young 35
We shared feelings

I asked her
What do you really need?
She replied
Slow loving sex

I broadly smiled
Took a deep breath
From a lady
What a strange request

Only men search for sex
The world is changing
What next?
A woman searching for sex.

She said I'm lonely
The beer doesn't help
I want to feel like a woman
Sex might help

I shook my head
I again smiled
Reluctantly said
Maybe I can help

We left the bar holding hands
Walked the sidewalk
Night lights shined
There was little talk

I asked
Are you sure?
She said I don't know
I want to try

We did

Near You

I'm not near you
Is it over?
Our love was strong
Now you are gone

We made love in the morning daylight
When it was quiet
I love you
I waited for the early light

I know you are a country guy
Said you could no longer live under the city lights
Longed for the openness
Why I can only guess

Took that pickup and drove away
Put your ring on the bed
I cried

What will I do?
I still love you
Let me join you

Watch the stars
Enjoy that early morning light
Make love again
Passionate love can again be ours

Don't let me just dream you
Live in these city lights
Show me your openness
Make love with me again

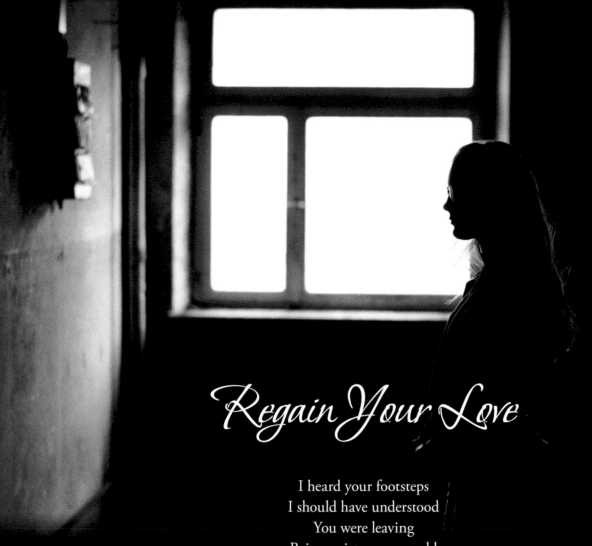

Regain Your Love

I heard your footsteps
I should have understood
You were leaving
Being quiet as you could

You didn't want me to know
Just leave with nowhere to go
You no longer feel the same
Just the pain

When did the aching start?
Will it ever end?
How will I know?
Will you tell me so?

I will come for you
No matter where you go
Try to regain your love
I should have understood

Love can quietly depart
Just leave the pain
Life moves in mysterious ways
Show me how to repair your broken heart
Impatiently step back through the door

Seasons Change

Our lives are like the turning world
In the Spring we play
Enjoy the cool
Make passionate love

Sit outside
Smile at one another
Drink a margarita
Nothing could be sweeter

Our love blossoms
Like the wildflowers
We feel young
Our love shall never come undone

In the Summer we feel the hot wind blow
Makes us move a bit more slow
Sweat trickles down our face
We persevere in any case

Look forward to the Fall
But time can cool our love
Begin to wilt like the wildflowers
Our life continues to turn

We yearn for what life can bring
Our love can change
Summer will not remain
Winter is not far away

It can bring feelings of regret
Cool passionate love
Freeze our longing
Forget how we met

Fall may make our love renew
Show us what can be true
The world is different
So are we

Turn, Turn, Turn
There is a season for every purpose
Under heaven
Seeger

Like the changing seasons
Our life changes
Life's Spring may not return

Southern Coking

I like that Southern food
Rejoice with those turnup greens
Relish the green beans
What a treat

The family joins me
Sit at the table
Look at those cloth napkin's
Miss the paper

They don't know true cuisine
It was known long ago
No longer with us

African slaves brought the bean's
Asia came with turnup greens
Others brought what they cherished
We call it southern food

It's cooked in a pot
Originally over flaming coals
The fire burned bright
Women watched the site

They stirred it with loving care
Knew what they could graciously share
We ate with smiling care
A delight

Southern cooking is right
It honors a long-suffering plight
Will we ever learn what is right?
Only if we relish how we live

Watched Love Die

What happened to our love?
It is no longer there
I loved you
You said you cared

Our lovie has changed
Does not remain
Disappeared slowly like the rain

We watched our love slowly die
We both cried
Something went wrong
We wonder why

I hold you but it's not the same
We once liked watching the rain
It's just not the same
We do not know why

Our love does not remain
Disappearing love is difficult to explain
It simply did not last
Like the rain

Through the years
Our love has not remained
We have grown apart
We do not think it can restart

Love may not last forever
Never return
Don't know why
We cannot explain

Wild Side

Shari has a wild side
Loves life
Wears her skirt in a personal way
Cares not what others say

Men never object
They just watch
Long to touch
Want to see more

Pixi hair with bangs
Bright red ruby lips
Shari has a wild side
It glows
She knows

She is not looking for a man
Just looks how she can
Does not hide

Holds her head high
The hair stays in place
Dose not hide her face
The lips shine

She is a different kind
Wild
She knows
Likes what she shows

Living wild is a different place
Moves at an exciting pace
Makes the world shine
I wish she were mine

She has a compelling wild side

You Were Gone

When I woke you were gone
I wondered why
When you were by the bed
I don't remember what you said

I threw back the covers
Struggled to stand
This must be a dream
A nightmare it seems

Where are you?
I want you here
Loving we could share
Come back

I heard the front door slam
I don't know why
I need to find my clothes
Find you and make things right

Why would you do this?
When you were by the bed
Tell me again what you said
I'm deeply confused

I don't know how to find you
I despair
Call me
I will come there

You can tell me what I've done wrong
What you want
I don't understand
I do care

Printed in the United States
By Bookmasters